Frogs
and Toads

Experts on child reading levels
have consulted on the level of text and
concepts in this book.

At the end of the book is a "Look Back and Find" section
which provides additional information and encourages
the child to refer back to previous pages
for the answers to the questions posed.

Published in the United States in 1985 by
Franklin Watts, 95 Madison Avenue, New York, NY 10016

© Aladdin Books Ltd/Franklin Watts

Designed and produced by
Aladdin Books Ltd, 28 Percy Street, London W1P 9FF

ISBN 0-531-10100-2

Printed in Belgium

FRANKLIN · WATTS · FIRST · LIBRARY

Frogs and Toads

by
Kate Petty

Consultant
Angela Grunsell

Illustrated by
Alan Baker

Franklin Watts
New York · London · Toronto · Sydney

Which is the frog and which is the toad?
This one is the grass frog. It is about two inches
long. Its shiny skin varies in color.
It can leap a long way on its strong back legs.

The toad often has a brown, warty skin.
It is usually bigger than a frog, with a
broader back. Unlike frogs, toads hop rather
slowly. They come out mostly at night.

The mother frog lays 2,000 to 4,000 eggs. The father holds her so that he can fertilize the eggs as soon as they are laid. The eggs look like little dots in a mass of jelly.

Can you see how toads' eggs are different? Over 10,000 eggs are laid in ribbons which wrap themselves around the water plants. Toads and frogs nearly always lay their eggs in water.

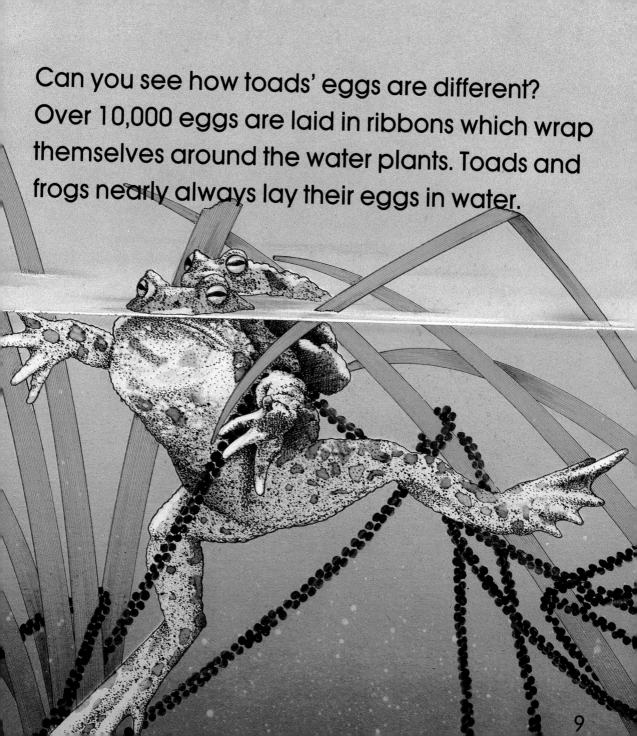

When the eggs hatch, thousands of tiny, wriggly tadpoles emerge from the jelly. Only a very few will survive long enough to become frogs. Other pond creatures like to eat tadpoles.

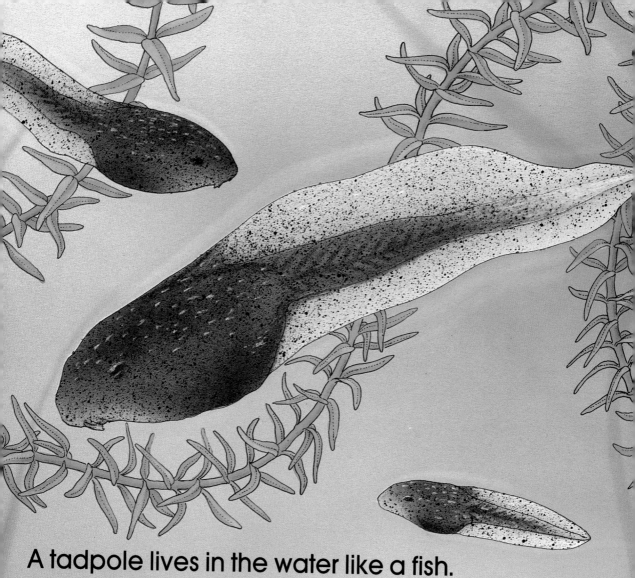

A tadpole lives in the water like a fish.
It breathes oxygen through the gills on the side
of its head. It moves by flicking its tail.
Small tadpoles feed off algae and pondweed.

11

Frogs and toads grow bigger in the same way.
They are getting ready for life out of the water.
By eight weeks the common toad tadpole has
lungs for breathing and a pair of back legs.

This little creature is really beginning
to look like a frog.
At ten weeks it has front legs with
"hands" and its tail is already shorter.

A baby frog is called a froglet. When it is strong enough it hops out of the water onto the land. Its powerful back legs with webbed feet are also good for swimming.

A full-grown frog is amphibious. This means
that it can live on land and in water.
A frog never lives too far away from water
as it needs to keep its skin moist.

A frog has eyes in the top of its head. It can peep out of the water without being seen. Frogs blink when they swallow. Their eyeballs push against their mouths to help the food down.

16

Frogs like to eat many kinds of insects. Toads are fond of ants and moths. They both catch all sorts of insects on their long sticky tongues. They cram food into their mouths with their "hands."

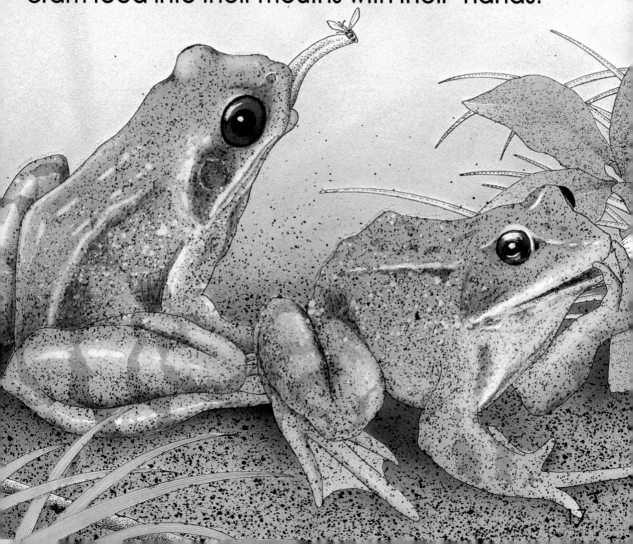

Have you ever heard frogs or toads croaking? Some kinds don't make much noise but others, like the spring peeper, can be heard a long way off. They puff out their throats like a balloon.

Only the male frogs and toads can croak.

They call and sing to their mates.

They can even croak under water.

This is a marine toad from Central America.

When a toad or frog is in danger, it can puff up its lungs and bow its head. This makes it harder for another animal to grab hold of it or try to swallow.

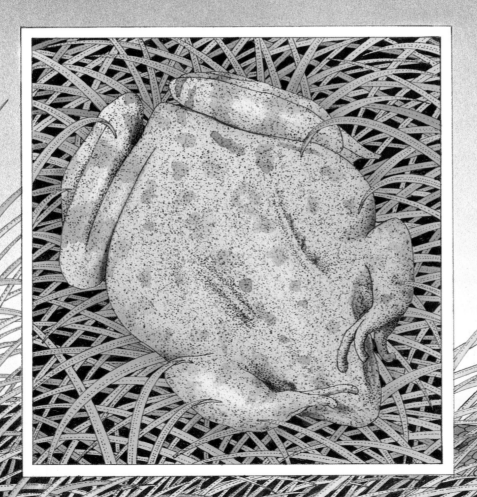

They also jack up their back legs. This makes them look much bigger and will scare off an enemy. Some toads and frogs give off a poison when attacked.

There are over 2,600 different frogs and toads known. Many of them are brightly colored and live in tropical countries, like these little tree frogs from Central America.

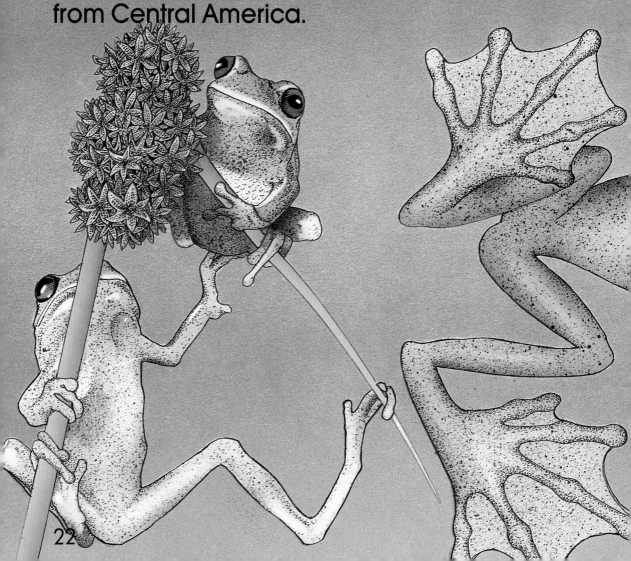

The flying frog from Asia
can glide from tree to tree.
Its webbed feet are like parachutes.
The reed frog from East Africa climbs up reeds

The male European midwife toad wraps the spawn around his legs and carries it about. The firebelly toad from Europe and Asia shows by its warning markings that it is poisonous.

When the spadesfoot toad is in danger
it just sinks from view, quietly digging
a hole with its back feet.

25

Most frogs and toads go to sleep for the winter. Frogs stay damp in the mud but you might find a toad sleeping in a barn or a cellar. In spring they go back to their ponds to mate.

Every spring thousands of toads and frogs cross busy roads on their way back. Helpers sometimes lift them across in buckets so that they can reach their breeding ponds in safety.

Look back and find

At what time of year do you find eggs?
In early spring.

What is the best way to study tadpoles?
*It is always best to study wildlife in its
own habitat, but you can take a cupful of
eggs and a little weed. Keep them in a large
aquarium filled with tap water.*

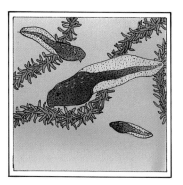

What do tadpoles eat in captivity?
*In the first two weeks the tadpoles can get
all they need from the weed and a few boiled
nettles. Then you can feed them on a little fish
food. Remember to change half the water once
a week. Once their back legs are fully formed
you should return them to the pond where their
natural diet helps them to grow into frogs.*

How do baby frogs and toads get ready for
land?

What happens to the tadpole's tail?
*It gets shorter and shorter and eventually
disappears.*

What is this toad doing?

Can all frogs and toads change color?
Most frogs and some toads can change color.
The common frog can be a different color
each time you see it, switching between
green and brown to match its surroundings.

Can frogs fly?
Not really. The flying frog takes
a tremendous leap and glides from one tree
to another.

Where does this frog come from?

What is special about its feet?

What is the firebelly doing?

Would you be poisoned if you touched its skin?
No, not unless you had cut yourself. Even the
common toad will make an unpleasant juice
come from its skin if it is frightened.

Index

A   amphibious 15

B   breathing

C   color 6, 7, 21, 22, 24
      croaking 18, 19

E   eating 11, 16, 17
      eggs 8, 9, 10
      eyes 16

F   feet 14, 25
      firebelly toad 24
      flying frog 23
      froglet 14

G   gills 11
      grass frog 6

H   hands 13, 17, 22

L   leap 6, 14
      legs 6, 12, 14, 25
      lungs 12, 13

M   marine toad 19
      midwife toad 25
      mouth 16, 17

P   poison 21, 24
      puffing up 20, 21

R   reed frog 18, 23
      roads 27

S   skin 6, 7, 15, 21
      sleep 11
      spadesfoot toad 25
      spring peeper 18
      swimming 14

T   tadpoles 10, 11, 12
      tail 11, 13
      tongue 17
      tree frog 22

W   webbed feet 14, 23